one-pot

simple and delicious easy-to-make recipes

Christine McFadden

p

This is a Parragon Publishing Book
This edition published in 2003

Parragon Publishing
Queen Street House
4 Queen Street
Bath, BA1 1HE, UK

ISBN: 1-40542-023-5

Printed in China

Produced by the Bridgewater Book Company Ltd.

Photographer Simon Punter

Home Economist Ricky Turner

Cover by 20 Twenty Design

NOTES FOR THE READER

- This book uses both imperial and metric measurements. Follow the same units of measurement throughout; do not mix imperial and metric.

- All spoon measurements are level: teaspoons are assumed to be 5 ml, and tablespoons are assumed to be 15 ml.

- Unless otherwise stated, milk is assumed to be whole milk, eggs and individual vegetables such as carrots are medium, and pepper is freshly ground black pepper.

- Recipes using raw eggs should be avoided by infants, the elderly, pregnant women, convalescents, and anyone suffering from an illness.

- The times given are an approximate guide only. Preparation times differ according to the techniques used by different people and the cooking times may also vary from those given. Optional ingredients, variations, or serving suggestions have not been included in the calculations.

contents

introduction

One-pot meals are the perfect solution for today's busy cooks. Whether it be a fortifying main-meal soup, an aromatic stew or casserole, or a hearty baked dish or gratin, a one-pot meal will look after itself while you do other things. They may not be fashionable food, but these are unpretentious, soul-satisfying dishes. They are also flexible as to timing, and can easily be kept waiting for late arrivals. And in most recipes, leftovers can be reheated, to taste even better next time around.

Each of these dishes is a self-contained meal, needing little accompaniment—perhaps just a simple salad and a hunk of bread. Because the food is cooked and served in a single pot, you will not be confronted with a pile of dirty dishes either.

To cook on top of the stove, you will need a medium-to-large pan with a heavy flat base which prevents the contents from sticking and burning. Depending on the recipe, stove-top meals can also be prepared in a heavy, high-sided skillet or sauté pan. For dishes that are started on top of the stove and finished in the oven, use a sturdy flameproof casserole or braising pan with ovenproof handles. All pans should have a well-fitting lid to keep the steam in and concentrate the flavors.

guide to recipe key		
	easy	Recipes are graded as follows: 1 pea = easy; 2 peas = very easy; 3 peas = extremely easy.
	serves 4	Recipes generally serve four people. Simply halve the ingredients to serve two, taking care not to mix imperial and metric measurements.
	20 minutes	Preparation time.
	1 hour	Cooking time.

speedy chili beef
page 24

spicy chicken hotpot
page 38

garbanzo bean & potato curry
page 72

brazilian seafood stew
page 88

meat one-pots

Thick, hearty soups, such as Scotch Broth or Winter Minestrone with Sausage, provide a nourishing meal-in-a-bowl, while the rich mellow flavors of traditional stews, such as Hungarian Goulash or Beef Bourgignon, will satisfy the most voracious of appetites. Chile-lovers will enjoy Speedy Chili Beef, as well as the robust spicy flavors of pork and beef in Mexican Meat Stew. There are also recipes for comforting casseroles and baked dishes with crisp toppings of garlic-flavored bread crumbs or bubbling cheese—perfect for a winter supper or weekend lunch.

winter minestrone
with sausage

		ingredients	
easy		3 tbsp olive oil	1 small red bell pepper, deseeded
		9 oz/250 g coarse-textured pork	and diced
serves 4		sausage, peeled and cut into chunks	3¾ cups chicken stock
		1 onion, sliced thinly	salt and pepper
		2 garlic cloves, chopped very finely	scant ½ cup short macaroni
		7 oz/200 g canned chopped tomatoes	generous ½ cup canned, drained
30 minutes		2 tbsp chopped fresh mixed herbs,	navy beans
		such as flat leaf parsley,	1 cup frozen peas
		sage, and marjoram	2 tbsp freshly grated Parmesan, plus
40 minutes		1 celery stalk, sliced thinly	extra to serve
		1 carrot, diced	4 thick slices Italian bread to serve

Heat the oil in a large pan over medium–low heat. Add the sausage and onion. Cook, stirring occasionally, until the onion is just colored.

Add the garlic, tomatoes, and herbs. Cook for 5 minutes, stirring. Add the celery, carrot, and bell pepper, cover, and cook the mixture for 5 minutes.

Pour in the stock. Bring to a boil, then cover, and simmer gently for 30 minutes.

Season with salt and pepper. Add the macaroni and beans and simmer for about 15 minutes, or until the macaroni is just tender.

Stir in the peas and cook for 5 minutes. Stir in the Parmesan.

To serve, place the bread in individual serving bowls. Ladle the soup over the bread and let stand for a few minutes. Serve with plenty of freshly grated Parmesan.

ham and root soup

		ingredients	
easy	2 tbsp vegetable oil	1 lb 12 oz/800 g peeled root	
	1 fresh bay leaf, shredded	vegetables, diced	
serves 4	1 tsp finely chopped fresh rosemary	4 cups chicken or ham stock	
	generous 1 cup diced ham	salt and pepper	
	1 large onion, chopped finely		
	2 celery stalks, diced	chopped fresh chives, to garnish	
20 minutes			
1 hour			

Heat the oil with the bay leaf and rosemary in a large pan over medium heat. Add the ham and stir-fry for a few minutes, or until beginning to crisp around the edges. Remove with a slotted spoon and set aside.

Add the onion, celery, and root vegetables to the pan. Stir well, then cover, and cook over medium–low heat for 15 minutes.

Pour in the stock. Bring to a boil, then simmer, partially covered, for 30 minutes.

Process about half the mixture in a blender or food processor, leaving the rest in the pan. Pour the purée back into the pan. Stir in the ham and cook over medium–low heat until heated through.

Season with salt, bearing in mind the saltiness of the ham, and freshly ground black pepper. Sprinkle with chopped chives and serve immediately.

scotch broth

		ingredients	
✎	very easy	1 large onion, quartered	1 small celery root, cut into chunks
		6 lamb shanks, weighing about	3 leeks, halved lengthwise and
🍴	serves 6	3 lb 8 oz/1.6 kg	sliced thickly
		1 garlic bulb, unpeeled, the outer	3 sprigs fresh thyme
		loose layers removed	1 fresh bay leaf
🥄	30 minutes	1 tbsp vegetable oil	1 tsp salt
		4 strips unsmoked bacon, diced	1 tsp pepper
		1 large onion, diced	3³⁄₄ cups chicken or beef stock
🕐	2 hours	3 carrots, sliced	¹⁄₄ cup pearl barley
	15 minutes	1 small rutabaga, cut into chunks	4 tbsp chopped fresh parsley

Heat the oven to 450°F/230°C. Roast the quartered onion, lamb, and garlic in a roasting pan for 30 minutes, or until well browned, turning occasionally. Turn into a large heavy pan. Pour in water to cover. Slowly bring to a boil, skimming off any foam. Cook over low heat, partially covered, for 1¼ hours.

Crisp the bacon in the oil in a large pan. Add the onion, vegetables, herbs, and seasoning. Pour in the the stock and add the barley. Bring to a boil, then simmer 35–40 minutes.

Remove the lamb and garlic from the first pan with a slotted spoon. Strip the meat from the bones and squeeze out the garlic pulp. Line a strainer with paper towels. Strain the lamb cooking liquid into a bowl. Blot up any surface fat with paper towels. Add 3 cups of the strained liquid, with the meat and garlic pulp, to the vegetables in the pan. Bring to a boil, then simmer for 10 minutes. Stir in the parsley just before serving.

mexican meat stew

	ingredients	
extremely easy	3 tbsp vegetable oil	3 tbsp lemon juice
	1 lb/450 g stewing beef, cubed	½ cup beef stock
	1 lb/450 g boneless pork, cubed	4 tbsp chopped fresh parsley
serves 4	1 onion, chopped finely	1 tsp ground cumin
	1 red bell pepper, deseeded	½ tsp dried oregano
	and chopped	½ tsp sugar
30 minutes	2–4 green chiles, deseeded and	salt and pepper
	chopped finely	
	2 garlic cloves, chopped very finely	3 tbsp chopped fresh cilantro,
3 hours	2 lb 10 oz/1.2 kg canned	to garnish
	chopped tomatoes	plain boiled rice, to serve

Heat the oil in a large flameproof casserole over medium–high heat. Add the meat in batches and cook until browned on all sides. Remove each batch with a slotted spoon, transfer to a bowl and set aside.

Add the onion and bell pepper and cook for 5 minutes, or until soft. Add the chiles and garlic and cook until the garlic is just colored. Return the meat and any juices to the casserole.

Add all the remaining ingredients, except the cilantro. Bring to a boil, stirring. Cover and simmer over low heat for 2 hours, stirring occasionally.

Remove the lid and simmer for 30–40 minutes, or until the sauce has thickened and the meat is very tender. Taste and add more salt if necessary.

Garnish with the cilantro just before serving. Serve with rice.

hungarian beef goulash

		ingredients	
extremely easy		2 tbsp vegetable oil	generous 1 cup beef stock
		1 lb 8 oz/675 g stewing beef, cubed	1 fresh bay leaf
serves 4		3 onions, chopped finely	3 tbsp chopped fresh parsley
		1 green bell pepper, deseeded	1 tbsp paprika
		and diced	1 tsp salt
30 minutes		2 garlic cloves, chopped very finely	¼ tsp pepper
		2 tbsp tomato paste	
		2 tbsp all-purpose flour	TO SERVE
3 hours		14 oz/400 g canned	buttered noodles
		chopped tomatoes	sour cream

Heat the oil in a flameproof casserole over medium–high heat. Add the meat and fry until evenly browned. Remove with a slotted spoon, transfer to a bowl, and set aside.

Add the onions and bell pepper. Cook for 5 minutes, stirring occasionally, until softened. Add the garlic and cook until just colored. Stir in the tomato paste and flour. Cook for 1 minute, stirring constantly.

Return the meat to the pan. Add the remaining ingredients and bring to a boil. Cover and simmer over low heat for 2½ hours, stirring occasionally. Add water or more stock if necessary.

Remove the lid and simmer, stirring to prevent the goulash from sticking, for 15 minutes, until the sauce has thickened and the meat is very tender.

Serve with buttered noodles and a bowl of sour cream.

beef bourguignon

		ingredients	
	very easy	6 oz/175 g piece unsmoked bacon, sliced into thin strips	3 cups red wine
	serves 6	2 tbsp olive oil	$1\frac{1}{2}$–2 cups beef stock
		3 lb/1.3 kg stewing beef, cut into 2 inch/5 cm pieces	bouquet garni
		2 carrots, sliced	1 tsp salt
	40 minutes	2 onions, chopped	$\frac{1}{4}$ tsp pepper
		2 garlic cloves, chopped very finely	3 tbsp butter
		3 tbsp all-purpose flour	12 oz/350 g pearl onions
	3 hours 15 minutes		$4\frac{3}{4}$ cups white mushrooms
			2 tbsp chopped fresh parsley

Lightly brown the bacon in the oil in a large casserole
(2–3 minutes). Remove with a slotted spoon. Brown the beef in
batches, drain, and keep with the bacon. Soften the carrots and
chopped onions in the same pan for 5 minutes. Add the garlic and
cook until just colored. Return the meat and bacon to the pan.
Sprinkle in the flour and cook for 1 minute, stirring. Add the wine
and enough stock to cover, the bouquet garni, salt, and pepper.
Bring to a boil, cover, and simmer gently for 3 hours.

Cook the pearl onions until soft in a covered skillet in half the
butter. Remove with a slotted spoon and keep warm. Cook the
mushrooms in the remaining butter. Remove and keep warm.

Strain the casserole liquid into a pan. Wipe the casserole and tip in
the meat, bacon, mushrooms, and onions. Remove the surface fat
from the cooking liquid, simmer for 1–2 minutes to reduce, and
pour it over the meat and vegetables. Serve sprinkled with parsley.

sausage
& tomato hotpot

		ingredients	
easy		2 tbsp olive oil	2 tsp chopped fresh rosemary
		8 oz/225 g coarse-textured pure pork	2 tsp chopped fresh thyme or oregano
serves 4		sausage, peeled and cut into chunks	2 lb 10 oz/1.2 kg canned
		2 onions, chopped finely	chopped tomatoes
		4 carrots, sliced thickly	salt and pepper
		6 potatoes, cut into chunks	
20 minutes		2 large garlic cloves, chopped	2 tbsp chopped fresh flat leaf parsley,
		very finely	to garnish
1 hour			

Heat the oil in a large, heavy pan over medium–high heat. Add the sausage and cook until browned. Remove from the pan with a slotted spoon and set aside.

Reduce the heat to medium. Add the onions, carrots, potatoes, garlic, rosemary, and thyme to the pan. Cover and cook gently for 10 minutes, stirring occasionally.

Return the sausage to the pan. Pour in the tomatoes and bring to a boil. Season with salt and pepper. Cover and simmer over medium–low heat, stirring occasionally, for 45 minutes until the vegetables are tender.

Sprinkle with the parsley just before serving.

beef pot roast
with potatoes & dill

very easy	
serves 6	
40 minutes	
3 hours 30 minutes	

ingredients

2½ tbsp all-purpose flour
1 tsp salt
¼ tsp pepper
3 lb 8 oz/1.6 kg rolled brisket
2 tbsp vegetable oil
2 tbsp butter
1 onion, chopped finely
2 celery stalks, diced

2 carrots, diced
1 tsp dill seed
1 tsp dried thyme or oregano
1½ cups red wine
generous 1 cup beef stock
4 or 5 potatoes, cut into large chunks
   and boiled until just tender
2 tbsp chopped fresh dill

Mix 2 tablespoons of flour with the salt and pepper in a shallow dish. Dip the meat to coat. Heat the oil in a casserole and brown the meat all over. Transfer to a plate. Add 1 tablespoon of butter to the casserole and cook the onion, celery, carrots, dill seed, and thyme for 5 minutes. Return the meat and juices to the pan.

Pour in the wine and enough stock to reach one-third of the way up the meat. Bring to a boil, cover, and cook for 3 hours in a preheated oven at 275°F/140°C, turning every half hour. After 2 hours, add the potatoes and more stock if needed.

When ready, transfer the meat and vegetables to a warm serving dish. Strain the cooking liquid into a pan.

Mix the remaining butter and flour to a paste. Bring the cooking liquid to a boil. Whisk in small pieces of the flour/butter paste, whisking until the sauce is smooth. Pour the sauce over the meat and vegetables. Sprinkle with the dill to serve.

speedy chili beef

		ingredients	
	extremely easy	3 tbsp vegetable oil	14 oz/400 g canned red kidney beans,
		1 lb/450 g ground beef	drained and rinsed
	serves 4	1 onion, chopped finely	1 tsp ground cumin
		1 green bell pepper, deseeded	1 tsp salt
		and diced	1 tsp sugar
	15 minutes	2 garlic cloves, chopped very finely	1–3 tsp chili powder
		1 lb 12 oz/800 g canned	2 tbsp chopped fresh cilantro
		chopped tomatoes	
	45 minutes		

Heat the oil in a large flameproof casserole over medium–high heat. Add the beef and cook, stirring, until lightly browned.

Reduce the heat to medium. Add the onion, bell pepper, and garlic. Cook for 5 minutes, or until soft.

Stir in the remaining ingredients. Bring to a boil. Simmer over medium–low heat, stirring frequently, for 30 minutes.

Stir in the cilantro just before serving.

beef, mushroom
& rice casserole

		ingredients	
	extremely easy	3 tbsp olive oil	2¼ cups sliced mushrooms
		14 oz/400 g ground beef	2 tbsp tomato paste
	serves 4	1 onion, chopped finely	1¼ cups long grain rice
		1 bell pepper, deseeded and	2½ cups hot beef stock
		chopped finely	salt and pepper
	15 minutes		scant ¾ cup freshly grated Cheddar
	35 minutes		

Heat the oil in a high-sided, lidded casserole over medium–high heat. Add the beef and cook, stirring, until lightly browned.

Reduce the heat to medium. Add the onion, bell pepper, mushrooms, and tomato paste. Cook for 5 minutes, or until soft.

Stir in the rice. Cook gently, stirring, for 3–4 minutes.

Pour in the hot stock. Season with salt and pepper. Bring to a boil. Cover tightly and simmer over low heat for about 20 minutes, or until the rice is tender and has absorbed most of the liquid.

Sprinkle with the cheese. Cover and let stand while the cheese melts. Serve immediately, straight from the dish.

spanish ham
& rice one-pot

		ingredients	
very easy		2 tbsp olive oil	14 oz/400 g canned
		1 onion, chopped finely	chopped tomatoes
serves 4		1 red bell pepper, deseeded and	1 cup long grain rice
		chopped finely	2 cups hot chicken stock
		12 oz/350 g piece of ham, cubed	salt and pepper
15 minutes		2 tsp paprika	¾ cup frozen peas
35 minutes			

Heat the oil in a large heavy pan over medium heat. Add the onion and bell pepper. Cook for 5 minutes, or until soft.

Stir in the ham, paprika, tomatoes, and rice. Cook, stirring constantly, for 3–4 minutes.

Pour in the hot stock. Season with salt and pepper. Bring to a boil. Cover tightly and simmer over low heat for 15 minutes.

Add the peas. Cover and cook for another 5 minutes, or until the rice is tender and has absorbed most of the liquid.

Remove the pan from the heat and let the dish stand for 5 minutes before serving.

lamb, garlic
& bean casserole

		ingredients	
	very easy	2 tbsp olive oil, plus extra for drizzling	½ tsp pepper
		2 lb/900 g boneless lamb, cut into	2½ cups chicken or lamb stock
	serves 4	1½ inch/4 cm cubes	1¼ cup dried cannellini or navy beans,
		2 onions, chopped finely	soaked overnight and drained
		1 tbsp chopped fresh rosemary	salt, to taste
	45 minutes	12 large garlic cloves, peeled and	1⅔ cups stale, coarse bread crumbs
		left whole	
		2 or 3 anchovy fillets,	chopped fresh flat leaf parsley,
	2 hours	chopped roughly	to garnish
	30 minutes	2 tbsp all-purpose flour	

Heat 1 tablespoon of the oil in a flameproof casserole. When very hot, cook the lamb in batches until evenly browned. Transfer to a plate. Cook the onion and rosemary in the remaining oil in the casserole for 5–7 minutes, stirring, until golden brown. Reduce the heat, stir in the garlic and anchovies, and cook for 1 minute.

Preheat the oven to 300°F/150°C. Return the meat and any juices from the plate to the casserole. Sprinkle in the flour and stir well. Season with the pepper. Pour in the stock, stirring constantly. Add the drained beans.

Bring to a boil, cover tightly, and cook in the preheated oven for 2 hours, or until soft. Remove from the oven. Season with salt.

Spread the bread crumbs over the lamb and beans. Drizzle a little olive oil over the top. Place under a preheated broiler for a few minutes until the crumbs are golden brown. Sprinkle with parsley and serve immediately.

poultry one-pots

Versatile poultry forms the basis of a wealth of one-pot meals. Chicken features widely in appetizing main-meal soups, spicy stews and hotpots, and easily prepared bean and rice dishes. To get the taste buds tingling, try Spicy Chicken Hotpot or New Orleans-style Chicken Jambalaya. Sweet and meaty duck goes Asian in a richly flavored stew of shiitake mushrooms and water chestnuts. Turkey is the main ingredient in what must be the speediest one-pot meal of all—a stir-fry of vibrant green snow peas and bok choy.

chicken, squash & spinach soup

		ingredients	
easy		1 tbsp olive oil	14 oz/400 g canned garbanzo beans,
		1 tbsp butter	drained and rinsed
serves 4		3 boneless, skinless chicken breast	¼ tsp ground cumin
		portions, cubed	salt and pepper
		2 small leeks, green part included,	4 cups chicken stock
		sliced thinly	4 oz/115 g baby spinach,
20 minutes		1 small butternut squash, cut into	chopped coarsely
		¾ inch/2 cm cubes	
		1 small green chile (optional),	warm crusty bread, to serve
1 hour		deseeded and chopped very finely	

Heat the oil and butter in a large pan over medium–low heat.
Add the chicken, leeks, squash, and chile, if using. Cover and
cook for 10 minutes, stirring occasionally, until the vegetables
are beginning to soften.

Add the garbanzo beans, cumin, salt, and pepper.

Pour in the stock. Bring to a boil, then simmer over low heat
for 40 minutes, or until the squash is tender.

Stir in the spinach. Cook for a few more minutes until the spinach
is just wilted, and serve with warm, crusty bread while piping hot.

chicken, sausage & bean stew

		ingredients	
	easy	2 tbsp vegetable oil	¼–½ tsp dried chili flakes
		4 boneless, skinless chicken breast	14 oz/400 g canned
	serves 4	portions, cubed	chopped tomatoes
		8 oz/225 g coarse-textured pork	14 oz/400 g canned cannellini beans,
		sausage, cut into large chunks	drained and rinsed
		4 frankfurter sausages, halved	⅔ cup chicken stock
	35 minutes	1 onion, chopped finely	salt and pepper
		3 carrots, sliced finely	
		1 garlic clove, chopped very finely	chopped fresh flat leaf parsley,
	45 minutes	1 tsp dried thyme	to garnish

Heat the oil in a large, heavy pan over medium–high heat. Cook the chicken, pork sausage, and frankfurters until lightly browned. Reduce the heat to medium. Add the onion and carrots. Cook for 5 minutes, or until soft.

Stir in the garlic, thyme, and chili flakes. Cook for 1 minute. Add the tomatoes, beans, and chicken stock. Season with salt and pepper. Bring to a boil, then simmer over low heat for 20–30 minutes, stirring occasionally.

Garnish with parsley just before serving.

spicy chicken hotpot

		ingredients	
very easy	2 tbsp vegetable oil	1 or 2 red chiles, deseeded and
	1 lb 5 oz/600 g skinless, boneless	chopped finely
serves 4	chicken breast portions, cubed	1 tsp salt
	1 tsp cumin seeds, crushed	$\frac{1}{4}$ tsp pepper
	2 tsp coriander seeds, crushed	14 oz/400 g canned
	2 tsp dried oregano or thyme	chopped tomatoes
45 minutes	1 onion, chopped	2 cups chicken stock
	2 potatoes, cubed	6 oz/175 g green beans, cut
	2 sweet potatoes, cubed	into 1$\frac{1}{2}$ inch/4 cm pieces
1 hour	3 carrots, sliced thickly	8 x frozen corn cob quarters
15 minutes	3 garlic cloves, chopped very finely	chopped fresh cilantro, to garnish

Heat the oil in a casserole over medium–high heat. Cook the chicken until lightly browned, stirring frequently. Stir in the cumin seeds, coriander seeds, and oregano. Cook for 1 minute.

Reduce the heat to medium. Add the onion, potatoes, sweet potatoes, carrots, garlic, and chiles. Cover and cook for 10 minutes, stirring occasionally, until beginning to soften.

Add the salt and pepper. Pour in the tomatoes and stock. Bring to a boil, cover, and simmer over medium–low heat for 30 minutes.

Add the beans and corn. Cook for 15 minutes more, or until the beans are just tender.

Garnish with cilantro just before serving.

chicken, beans
& spinach with olives

		ingredients	
very easy	2 tbsp olive oil	14 oz/400 g canned cannellini beans,
	1 lb 5 oz/600 g skinless, boneless	drained and rinsed
serves 4	chicken breast portions, cut	generous 1 cup chicken stock
	into chunks	salt and pepper
	1 small onion, chopped finely	12 oz/350 g baby spinach,
	2 celery stalks, diced	chopped roughly
20 minutes	3 large garlic cloves, chopped finely	
	2 tsp chopped fresh rosemary	8–10 pitted black olives (sliced),
	¼ tsp dried chili flakes	to garnish
45 minutes	14 oz/400 g canned	
	chopped tomatoes	

Heat the oil in a casserole over medium–high heat. Cook the chicken until lightly browned, stirring frequently.

Reduce the heat to medium. Add the onion and celery. Cook for 5 minutes, or until soft.

Stir in the garlic, rosemary, and chili flakes. Cook for another minute. Add the tomatoes, beans, and chicken stock. Season with salt and pepper.

Bring to a boil, then simmer over medium–low heat for 20 minutes. Stir in the spinach. Cook for about 3 minutes, or until wilted.

Garnish with the olives and serve immediately.

chicken with rice, mushrooms & tomatoes

	very easy	
	serves 4	
	15 minutes	
	1 hour	

ingredients

2 tbsp olive oil
1 lb 7 oz/650 g boneless, skinless
   chicken breast portions, cubed
1 onion, chopped finely
1⅔ cups finely sliced mushrooms
2 garlic cloves, chopped very finely

4 tbsp chopped fresh flat leaf parsley
1¾ cups long grain rice
14 oz/400 g canned
   chopped tomatoes
salt and pepper
2 cups hot chicken stock

Heat the oil in a large, heavy skillet over medium–high heat. Cook the chicken until lightly browned, stirring frequently.

Reduce the heat to medium. Add the onion and mushrooms. Cook for 5 minutes, or until soft. Stir in the garlic and 2 tablespoons of the parsley. Cook for 1 minute.

Add the rice and cook for 5 minutes, stirring constantly. Add the tomatoes. Season with salt and pepper. Cook for another minute. Stir in the hot stock. Bring to a boil, then cover tightly, and simmer over low heat for 20–25 minutes, or until the rice is tender.

Remove from the heat and let the dish stand, covered, for 10 minutes before serving. Sprinkle with the remaining parsley to garnish and serve.

chicken jambalaya

		ingredients	
	easy	3 tbsp vegetable oil	1 tsp dried oregano
		900 g/2 lb boneless, skinless	¼ tsp dried chili flakes
	serves 4	chicken thighs	8 oz/225 g chorizo sausage,
		1 onion, chopped finely	cut into chunks
		2 red or green bell peppers, deseeded	3 plum tomatoes, chopped roughly
		and chopped finely	salt and pepper
	30 minutes	2 garlic cloves, chopped very finely	2½ cups hot chicken stock
		1½ cups long grain rice	3 scallions, green part included,
		2 tbsp tomato paste	chopped finely
	1 hour 10 minutes	1 tsp dried thyme	

Heat the oil in a flameproof casserole over medium–high heat. Cook the chicken in batches until lightly browned, stirring frequently. Remove each batch with a slotted spoon and transfer to a plate.

Reduce the heat to medium. Add the onion and bell peppers. Cook for 5 minutes, or until soft. Add the garlic and cook for 1 minute. Add the rice and cook for 5 minutes, stirring constantly.

Add the tomato paste, thyme, oregano, chili flakes, chorizo, and tomatoes. Season with salt and pepper. Cook for 2–3 minutes.

Return the chicken and any juices to the casserole. Stir in the hot stock. Bring to a boil, then cover tightly, and simmer over low heat for 20–25 minutes, or until the rice is tender.

Remove from the heat. Sprinkle with the scallions. Cover and let stand for 10 minutes before serving.

braised asian duck

		ingredients	
	very easy	3 tbsp soy sauce	2 tbsp rice wine or dry sherry
		¼ tsp Chinese five-spice powder	1 tbsp oyster sauce
	serves 4	¼ tsp pepper	3 whole star anise
		pinch of salt	2 tsp black peppercorns
		4 duck legs or breasts, cut into pieces	2–2½ cups chicken stock or water
		3 tbsp vegetable oil	6 dried shiitake mushrooms, soaked in
	30 minutes	1 tsp dark sesame oil	warm water for 20 minutes
		1 tsp finely chopped fresh ginger root	8 oz/225 g canned water chestnuts,
		1 large garlic clove, finely chopped	drained and rinsed
	2 hours	4 scallions, white part sliced thickly,	2 tbsp cornstarch
		green part shredded	

Combine 1 tablespoon of the soy sauce, the five-spice powder, pepper, and salt and rub over the duck pieces. Brown the pieces in 2½ tablespoons of vegetable oil, remove, and transfer to a plate.

Drain the fat from the casserole and wipe out. Heat the sesame oil and remaining vegetable oil. Add the ginger and garlic. Cook for a few seconds. Add the white scallion. Cook for a few seconds. Return the duck to the pan. Add the rice wine, oyster sauce, star anise, peppercorns, and remaining soy sauce. Pour in just enough stock to cover. Bring to a boil, cover, and simmer gently for 1½ hours, adding more water if necessary.

Drain the mushrooms and squeeze dry. Slice the caps and add to the duck with the water chestnuts. Simmer for 20 minutes more.

Mix the cornstarch with 2 tablespoons of the cooking liquid to a smooth paste. Add to the remaining liquid, stirring until thickened. Garnish with the green scallion shreds to serve.

turkey stir-fry
with noodles

		ingredients	
easy	8 oz/225 g dried egg noodles	1½ cups snow peas,
	9 oz/250 g turkey scallops,	halved lengthwise
	cut into thin strips	8 oz/225 g bok choy, cut into
serves 4	1 tsp cornstarch	½ inch/1 cm diagonal slices
	1 tsp sugar	6 thin slices fresh ginger root,
	¼ tsp salt	chopped very finely
20 minutes	3 tbsp soy sauce	1 large garlic clove, chopped
	3 tbsp vegetable oil	very finely
	2 tbsp dark sesame oil	salt and pepper
20 minutes	6–8 shiitake mushrooms, sliced finely	

Cook the noodles according to the packet instructions. Drain, rinse with cold water, and set aside.

Spread the turkey strips on a plate. Dredge with the cornstarch, sugar, salt, and soy sauce. Toss well to coat.

Heat 2 tablespoons of vegetable oil and 1 tablespoon of sesame oil in a wok or large skillet over high heat. When very hot, add the turkey. Stir-fry for 2 minutes. Add the mushrooms, snow peas, and bok choy. Stir-fry for 2 minutes. Add the ginger and garlic. Stir-fry for 1 minute. Season with salt and pepper. Transfer the turkey and vegetables to a warm dish.

Reduce the heat to medium. Add the remaining oils to the wok or skillet. When hot, add the cooked noodles. Stir-fry for 2 minutes, or until heated through and thoroughly coated with oil. Return the turkey and vegetables to the pan. Mix with the noodles and serve immediately.

mexican chicken, chile & potato pot

		ingredients	
easy	2 tbsp vegetable oil	1 or 2 green chiles, deseeded and
	1 lb/450 g boneless, skinless chicken	chopped very finely
serves 4	breast portions, cubed	7 oz/200 g canned chopped tomatoes
	1 onion, chopped finely	½ tsp dried oregano
	1 green bell pepper, deseeded and	½ tsp salt
	chopped finely	¼ tsp pepper
30 minutes	1 potato, diced	4 tbsp chopped fresh cilantro
	1 sweet potato, diced	2 cups chicken stock
	2 garlic cloves, chopped very finely	
35 minutes		

Heat the oil in a large, heavy pan over medium–high heat. Cook the chicken until lightly browned.

Reduce the heat to medium. Add the onion, bell pepper, potato, and sweet potato. Cover and cook for 5 minutes, stirring occasionally, until the vegetables begin to soften.

Add the garlic and chiles. Cook for 1 minute. Stir in the tomatoes, oregano, salt, pepper, and 2 tablespoons of the cilantro. Cook for 1 minute.

Pour in the stock. Bring to a boil, then cover, and simmer over medium–low heat for 15–20 minutes, or until the chicken is cooked through and the vegetables are tender.

Sprinkle with the remaining cilantro just before serving.

paprika chicken
& rice casserole

		ingredients	
easy	3 tbsp vegetable oil	2 cups hot chicken stock	
	4 part-boned chicken breast portions,	2 tsp paprika	
serves 4	about 5½ oz/150 g each	2 tsp dried thyme	
	1 onion, chopped finely	salt and pepper	
	2 garlic cloves, chopped very finely	1½ cups coarsely grated Cheddar	
20 minutes	1 cup long grain rice	or mozzarella	
	10 oz/280 g frozen mixed vegetables		
1 hour			

Heat the oil in a shallow flameproof casserole over medium–high heat. Cook the chicken in batches until lightly browned. Remove with a slotted spoon and transfer to a plate.

Reduce the heat to medium. Add the onion. Cook for 5 minutes until soft. Add the garlic and cook for 1 minute. Stir in the rice and cook for 5 minutes, stirring constantly.

Add the frozen vegetables, hot stock, and 1 teaspoon each of the paprika and thyme. Bring to a boil, stirring until well mixed. Season with salt and pepper. Place the chicken on top of the rice mixture. Sprinkle with the remaining paprika and thyme.

Cover tightly and simmer over low heat for 20–25 minutes, or until the liquid is absorbed and the chicken cooked through.

Remove from the heat. Sprinkle with the cheese. Place under a preheated broiler for 5 minutes. Serve when the cheese has melted.

turkey, leek
& cheese gratin

		ingredients	
easy	1 cup short macaroni	1²⁄₃ cups diced cooked turkey
	1 medium egg, beaten lightly	or chicken
serves 4	2 tbsp butter	¹⁄₃ cup diced ham
	4 small leeks, green part included,	3 tbsp chopped fresh
	sliced finely	flat leaf parsley
	2 carrots, diced	salt and pepper
30 minutes	1 tbsp all-purpose flour	scant 1 cup freshly grated
	¼ tsp freshly grated nutmeg	Swiss cheese
	generous 1 cup chicken stock	
40 minutes		

Cook the macaroni in plenty of boiling salted water until just tender. Drain and return to the pan. Stir in the egg and a pat of the butter, mixing well. Set aside.

Preheat the oven to 350°F/180°C.

Melt the remaining butter in a pan over medium heat. Add the leeks and carrots. Cover and cook for 5 minutes, shaking the pan occasionally, until just tender.

Add the flour and nutmeg. Cook for 1 minute, stirring constantly. Pour in the stock. Bring to a boil, stirring constantly. Stir in the turkey, ham, and parsley. Season with salt and pepper.

Spread half the turkey mixture over the bottom of a shallow ovenproof dish. Spread the macaroni over the turkey. Top with the remaining turkey mixture. Sprinkle with the cheese.

Bake for 15–20 minutes. Serve when golden and bubbling.

vegetable one-pots

Vibrant vegetables combine with the earthy flavors of legumes, grains, and pasta in deeply satisfying and nutritious one-pot meals. All are simple to prepare and make exciting eating whatever the occasion— midweek suppers or entertaining friends. Try Barley & Bell Pepper Pilaf, or the colorful and crisp-textured Lentil & Rice Pilaf with Celery, Carrots & Orange—perfect for a festive vegetarian meal. Or experience the earthy, complex flavors of mushrooms and eggplants in Baked Mediterranean Vegetables with Feta.

hearty lentil
& vegetable soup

		ingredients	
very easy		2 tbsp vegetable oil	generous ⅓ cup long grain rice
		3 leeks, green part included,	4 cups chicken stock
serves 4		sliced finely	8 x corn cob quarters
		3 carrots, diced	salt and pepper
		2 celery stalks, quartered lengthwise	
15 minutes		and diced	TO SERVE
		½ cup brown or green lentils	4 tbsp chopped fresh chives
			sour cream
40 minutes			

Heat the oil in a large pan over medium heat. Add the leeks, carrots, and celery. Cover and cook for 5–7 minutes, or until just tender. Stir in the lentils and rice.

Pour in the stock. Bring to a boil, then cover, and simmer over medium–low heat for 20 minutes.

Add the corn. Simmer for 10 minutes more, or until the lentils and rice are tender.

Season with salt and pepper. Stir in the chives. Ladle into individual bowls, top with a spoonful of sour cream and serve immediately.

beans & greens soup

		ingredients	
	very easy	3 tbsp olive oil	14 oz/400 g canned borlotti beans,
		1 large white onion, sliced thinly	drained and rinsed
	serves 4	3 garlic cloves, chopped very finely	$3\frac{3}{4}$ cups chicken or
		2 or 3 mild green chiles, such as	vegetable stock
		Anaheim, deseeded and chopped	salt and pepper
		1 tsp dried oregano	
	30 minutes	$2\frac{3}{4}$ cups shredded savoy cabbage	3 tbsp chopped fresh cilantro,
		or kale	to garnish
	20 minutes		

Heat the oil in a large pan over medium heat. Cook the onion for 5–7 minutes, or until soft.

Add the garlic, chiles, and oregano. Cook for a few seconds, or until the garlic is just beginning to color. Add the cabbage, beans, and stock. Season with salt and pepper.

Bring to a boil, then cover, and simmer for 7–10 minutes or until the cabbage is just tender.

Sprinkle with the cilantro just before serving.

creamy potato,
onion & cheese soup

		ingredients	
very easy		3 tbsp butter	⅔ cup milk
		1 small onion, chopped finely	⅔ cup whipping cream
serves 4		6 scallions, green part included, chopped finely	3 tbsp chopped fresh parsley
			scant ¾ cup coarsely grated Cheddar
		4 potatoes, cut into chunks	
15 minutes		3 cups chicken stock	fried garlic croûtons (optional),
		salt and pepper	to serve
30 minutes			

Heat the butter in a large pan over medium heat. Add the onion, scallions, and potatoes. Cover and cook for 5–7 minutes until the onions are just tender.

Add the stock. Bring to a boil, then cover, and simmer over medium–low heat for 15–20 minutes, or until the potatoes are tender. Remove from the heat.

Mash the potatoes. Season with salt and pepper. Stir in the milk, cream, and 2 tablespoons of the parsley. Reheat gently. Ladle into bowls. Sprinkle with the cheese and remaining parsley.

Serve with the croûtons, if using.

tomato, mushroom & macaroni hotpot

		ingredients	
easy		3 tbsp olive oil	1lb 12 oz/800 g canned
		1 onion, sliced	chopped tomatoes
serves 4		generous 1 cup thinly	2 cups chicken stock
		sliced mushrooms	2 cups dried short macaroni
		2 garlic cloves, chopped very finely	1 tsp salt
20 minutes		1 tsp dried oregano	¼ tsp pepper
		2 tbsp tomato paste	
		3 tbsp chopped fresh	freshly grated Parmesan,
30 minutes		flat leaf parsley	to serve

Heat the olive oil in a large pan or high-sided skillet with a lid, over medium heat. Add the onion and mushrooms. Cook, stirring frequently, for 5–7 minutes, or until soft.

Stir in the garlic, oregano, tomato paste, and 1½ tablespoons of the parsley. Cook for 1 minute. Pour in the tomatoes and stock. Bring to a boil.

Add the macaroni, salt, and pepper. Bring back to a boil. Cover and simmer over medium–low heat for 20 minutes, stirring occasionally, or until the macaroni is tender.

Sprinkle with the remaining parsley just before serving. Serve with freshly grated Parmesan.

mexican three-bean
chili hotpot

		ingredients	
very easy		¾ cup each black beans, cannellini beans, and pinto beans, soaked overnight in separate bowls	1 tsp dried oregano
serves 6		2 tbsp olive oil	½–2 tsp chili powder
		1 large onion, chopped finely	3 tbsp tomato paste
30 minutes		2 red bell peppers, deseeded and diced	1 lb 12 oz/800 g canned chopped tomatoes
		2 garlic cloves, chopped very finely	1 tsp sugar
2 hours		½ tsp cumin seeds, crushed	1 tsp salt
		1 tsp coriander seeds, crushed	2½ cups chicken or vegetable stock
			3 tbsp chopped fresh cilantro

Drain the beans, put in separate pans, and cover with fresh water. Boil rapidly for 10–15 minutes, then simmer for 35–45 minutes, or until just tender. Drain and set aside.

Heat the oil in a large, heavy pan over medium heat. Cook the onion and bell peppers for 5 minutes, or until soft.

Stir in the garlic, cumin and coriander seeds, and oregano. Cook for a few seconds, or until the garlic is just beginning to color. Add the chili powder and tomato paste. Cook for 1 minute. Add the tomatoes, sugar, salt, beans, and stock. Stir well and bring to a boil. Cover and simmer over low heat for 45 minutes, stirring occasionally to prevent sticking.

Stir in the cilantro and remove from the heat. Ladle into individual bowls to serve.

barley & pepper pilaf

		ingredients	
easy	1 tbsp vegetable oil	3$\frac{1}{4}$ cups thinly sliced mushrooms
	2 tbsp butter	2 tbsp chopped fresh flat leaf parsley
serves 4	1 onion, chopped finely	2 garlic cloves, chopped very finely
	1 red bell pepper, deseeded and chopped finely	1$\frac{3}{4}$ cups pearl barley
25 minutes	1 green bell pepper, deseeded and chopped finely	1$\frac{3}{4}$–2$\frac{1}{2}$ cups chicken or vegetable stock
		salt and pepper
1 hour 15 minutes		

Heat the oil and butter in a high-sided skillet with a lid over medium heat. Add the onion, bell peppers, and mushrooms. Cook for 5–7 minutes, or until soft, stirring frequently.

Add the parsley and garlic. Cook for 1 minute. Add the pearl barley and mix well. Pour in 1¾ cups of the stock. Season with salt and pepper.

Stir, bring to a boil, then cover, and simmer over low heat for about 1 hour, or until the barley is tender and most of the liquid has been absorbed. Add more stock if necessary.

Remove from the heat and let stand for 5 minutes. Fluff with a fork before serving.

lentil & rice pilaf
with celery, carrots & orange

		ingredients	
	very easy	4 tbsp vegetable oil	⅓ cup whole almonds, sliced
		1 red onion, chopped finely	lengthwise
	serves 4	2 tender celery stalks, leaves included,	2 cups cooked brown
		quartered lengthwise and diced	basmati rice
		2 carrots, grated coarsely	⅔ cup cooked orange lentils
		1 green chile, deseeded and	¾ cup chicken or vegetable stock
	30 minutes	chopped finely	5 tbsp fresh orange juice
		3 scallions, green part included,	salt and pepper
		chopped finely	
	15 minutes		

Heat 2 tablespoons of the oil in a high-sided skillet with a lid over medium heat. Add the onion. Cook, stirring frequently, for 5 minutes, or until soft.

Add the celery, carrots, chile, scallions, and almonds. Stir-fry for 2 minutes, or until the vegetables are al dente, but still brightly colored. Transfer to a bowl and set aside.

Add the remaining oil to the pan. Stir in the rice and lentils. Cook over medium–high heat, stirring, for 1–2 minutes, or until heated through. Reduce the heat. Stir in the stock and orange juice. Season with salt and pepper.

Return the vegetables to the pan. Toss with the rice for a few minutes until heated through. Transfer to a warm dish to serve.

garbanzo bean & potato curry

		ingredients	
	easy	¾ cup garbanzo beans, soaked	½ tsp cayenne
		3 tbsp vegetable oil	2 tbsp tomato paste
	serves 6	½ tsp cumin seeds	14 oz/400 g canned
		½ tsp mustard seeds	chopped tomatoes
		1 onion, chopped finely	2 potatoes, cubed
		2 garlic cloves, chopped very finely	3 tbsp chopped fresh cilantro
	40 minutes	¾ inch/2 cm piece fresh ginger root,	1 tbsp lemon juice
		chopped very finely	1–1¼ cups chicken or vegetable stock
		1 tsp salt	thinly sliced white or red onion rings,
	2 hours	2 tsp ground coriander	and cooked rice, to serve
		1 tsp ground turmeric	

Boil the garbanzo beans rapidly in plenty of water for 15 minutes. Reduce the heat and boil gently for 1 hour, or until tender. Drain and set aside.

Heat the oil in a large pan or high-sided skillet. Stirring constantly, add the cumin and mustard seeds, cover, and cook for a few seconds, or until the seeds pop. Add the onion. Cover and cook for 3–5 minutes, or until just brown. Add the garlic and ginger. Cook for a few seconds. Stir in the salt, coriander, turmeric, and cayenne, then the tomato paste and tomatoes. Simmer for a few minutes. Add the garbanzo beans, potatoes, and 2 tablespoons of the chopped cilantro.

Stir in the lemon juice and 1 cup of the stock. Bring to a boil, then simmer for 30–40 minutes, or until the potatoes are cooked. Add more stock if the mixture becomes too dry.

Serve garnished with onion rings and the remaining cilantro.

baked mediterranean vegetables with feta

		ingredients	
	very easy	1 red onion, sliced into thick rings	1 tbsp chopped fresh flat leaf parsley
		1 small eggplant, sliced thickly	1 tsp chopped fresh rosemary
	serves 4	2 large mushrooms, halved	1 tsp dried thyme or oregano
		3 red bell peppers, halved	finely grated rind of 1 lemon
		and deseeded	generous 1 cup stale, coarse
		3 tbsp olive oil, plus extra for brushing	bread crumbs
	40 minutes	3 plum tomatoes, peeled and diced	6–8 black olives, pitted and sliced
		salt and pepper	1 oz/25 g feta, cut into
		2 garlic cloves, chopped very finely	½ inch/1 cm cubes
	40 minutes		

Put the onion, eggplant, mushrooms, and bell peppers on a large cookie sheet, placing the bell peppers cut side down. Oil lightly.

Broil for 10–12 minutes, turning the onion, eggplant, and mushrooms halfway through, until beginning to blacken. Cut into even-size chunks. Place in a shallow ovenproof dish. Arrange the diced tomatoes on top. Season with salt and pepper.

Preheat the oven to 425°F/220°C.

In a bowl, combine the garlic, parsley, rosemary, thyme, and lemon rind with the bread crumbs. Season with pepper. Add the 3 tablespoons of olive oil to bind the mixture together. Sprinkle the mixture over the vegetables. Add the olives and feta cheese.

Bake in the preheated oven for 10–15 minutes, or until the vegetables are heated through and the topping is crisp. Serve straight from the dish.

spinach, mushroom & rice gratin

		ingredients	
easy		1 tbsp olive oil	salt, to taste
		1 tbsp butter	450 g/1 lb spinach, stalks removed,
serves 4		1 onion, chopped finely	leaves sliced into thin ribbons
		3¼ cups thinly sliced mushrooms	1 cup long grain rice
		2 garlic cloves, chopped very finely	1¾ cups water
35 minutes		½ tsp dried thyme or oregano	¼–½ tsp pepper
		¼ tsp dried chili flakes	1 cup coarsely grated Edam or
		finely grated rind of ½ lemon	mild Cheddar
50 minutes			

Heat the oil and butter in a pan over medium heat. Add the onion and mushrooms. and cook for 5 minutes. Add the garlic, thyme, chili flakes, lemon rind, and salt to taste. Cook for a few seconds.

Add the spinach and stir until wilted. Stir in the rice and cook for a few minutes, or until the grains are translucent. Add the water and bring to a boil. Cover tightly and simmer over low heat for 15–20 minutes, or until the water has been absorbed.

Preheat the oven to 350°F/180°C.

Transfer the mixture to a lightly greased ovenproof dish. Season with the pepper. Sprinkle the cheese over the surface. Gently fork it into the rice.

Cover with foil. Bake in the preheated oven for about 20 minutes, until the cheese has melted.

Remove the foil and bake for 5 minutes more before serving.

eggplant gratin

		ingredients	
very easy		4 tbsp olive oil	salt and pepper
		2 onions, chopped finely	14 oz/400 g canned
serves 4 as		2 garlic cloves, chopped very finely	chopped tomatoes
an appetizer		2 eggplants, sliced thickly	1½ cups coarsely
		3 tbsp chopped fresh flat leaf parsley	grated mozzarella
15 minutes		½ tsp dried thyme	6 tbsp freshly grated Parmesan
40 minutes			

Heat the oil in a skillet over medium heat. Add the onion and cook for 5 minutes, or until soft. Add the garlic and cook for a few seconds, or until just beginning to color. Using a slotted spoon, transfer the onion mixture to a plate.

Cook the eggplant slices in batches in the same skillet until they are just lightly browned.

Preheat the oven to 400°F/200°C.

Arrange a layer of eggplant slices in the bottom of a shallow ovenproof dish. Sprinkle with the parsley, thyme, salt, and pepper. Add a layer of onion, tomatoes, and mozzarella, sprinkling parsley, thyme, salt, and pepper over each layer.

Continue layering, finishing with a layer of eggplant slices. Sprinkle with the Parmesan. Bake, uncovered, for 20–30 minutes, or until the top is golden and the eggplants are tender. Serve hot.

fish
one-pots

Easy to prepare and quick to cook, fish and
shellfish make mouthwatering one-pot
meals. Fresh or frozen, bottled or canned,
a variety of fish and shellfish can go into
the pot. Firm-fleshed white fish, such as cod
or snapper, are ideal since they maintain
texture and succulence while gently
simmering in a sauce. Plump, juicy shrimp,
briny clams, scallops, and mussels also
provide a taste of the ocean. The recipes
include a Brazilian shellfish stew, redolent
with saffron, as well as rich, creamy
chowders and a Cajun-style gumbo.

fish & shellfish chowder

		ingredients	
very easy		1 tsp vegetable oil	salt and pepper
		4 strips lean bacon	5 cups hot milk
serves 4		4 tbsp butter	12 oz/350 g firm white fish,
		1 large onion, chopped finely	such as cod, haddock, or hake,
		2 celery stalks, quartered lengthwise	cut into chunks
		and diced	10 oz/280 g clams (in jar)
40 minutes		3 mealy potatoes, cubed	6–8 peeled jumbo shrimp, halved
		3 tbsp chopped fresh parsley	6 large scallops (optional),
		1 tsp chopped fresh thyme	sliced thickly
40 minutes		1 fresh bay leaf	

Heat the oil in a skillet over medium–high heat. Cook the bacon until crisp. Drain on paper towels, crumble into bite-size pieces, and set aside.

Heat the butter in a large pan. Add the onion, celery, and potatoes. Reduce the heat to medium–low. Cover and cook for 10 minutes, stirring occasionally, until beginning to soften.

Add 2 tablespoons of the parsley, the thyme, and bay leaf. Season generously with salt and pepper. Pour in the hot milk. Cover and simmer for 15 minutes. Add the fish and continue cooking for 5 minutes.

Add the clams and their juice, the shrimp, and scallops, if using. Simmer for 5 minutes more.

Ladle into individual bowls. Serve garnished with the bacon pieces and the remaining parsley.

caribbean fish chowder

		ingredients	
very easy		3 tbsp vegetable oil	4 cups chicken stock
		1 tsp cumin seeds, crushed	salt and pepper
		1 tsp dried thyme or oregano	14 oz/400 g red snapper fillets,
serves 4		1 white onion, diced	cut into chunks
		½ green bell pepper, deseeded	¼ cup frozen peas
		and diced	3 tbsp frozen corn kernels
35 minutes		1 sweet potato, diced	½ cup light cream
		2 or 3 green chiles, deseeded and	
		very finely chopped	3 tbsp chopped fresh cilantro,
45 minutes		1 garlic clove, chopped very finely	to garnish

Heat the oil with the cumin seeds and thyme in a large pan over medium heat. Add the onion, bell pepper, sweet potato, chiles, and garlic. Cook, stirring, for 1 minute.

Reduce the heat to medium–low. Cover and cook for 10 minutes, or until beginning to soften.

Pour in the chicken stock. Season generously with salt and pepper. Bring to a boil, then cover, and simmer over medium–low heat for 20 minutes.

Add the red snapper, peas, corn, and cream. Cook, uncovered, for 7–10 minutes, or until the fish is cooked.

Stir in the cilantro to garnish just before serving.

shrimp gumbo

		ingredients	
very easy		2 tbsp vegetable oil	½ tsp dried thyme or oregano
		2 tbsp butter	1 fresh bay leaf
serves 4		9 oz/250 g ladies' fingers, trimmed and sliced thickly	salt and pepper
		1 white onion, chopped finely	3¾ cups chicken stock or water
40 minutes		2 celery stalks, quartered lengthwise and diced	4 cups peeled fresh or frozen raw shrimp
		1 green bell pepper, deseeded and diced	few drops of Tabasco sauce
45 minutes		2 garlic cloves, chopped very finely	2 tbsp chopped fresh cilantro, to garnish
		7 oz/200 g canned chopped tomatoes	

Heat the oil and butter in a large pan over medium heat. Add the ladies' fingers and cook, uncovered, for 15 minutes, or until they lose their sticky consistency.

Add the onion, celery, bell pepper, garlic, tomatoes, thyme, and bay leaf. Season with salt and pepper. Cover and cook over medium–low heat for 10 minutes.

Pour in the stock. Bring to a boil, then cover, and simmer over medium–low heat for 15 minutes, or until the vegetables are al dente. Add the shrimp and Tabasco sauce. Cook for about 5 minutes, or until the shrimp are pink.

Stir in the cilantro to garnish just before serving.

brazilian shellfish stew

		ingredients	
easy		1 lb/450 g mussels, scrubbed	salt and pepper
		2 tbsp olive oil	2 lb/900 g cod steaks, cut into chunks
serves 4		1 onion, chopped finely	8 oz/225 g raw jumbo shrimp, peeled
		2 garlic cloves, chopped very finely	7 oz/200 g canned crab meat
		14 oz/400 g canned	7 oz/200 g clams (in jar)
30 minutes		chopped tomatoes	
		¼ tsp cayenne	3 tbsp chopped fresh cilantro,
		pinch of saffron threads	to garnish
35 minutes			

Remove the "beards" from the mussels. Rinse the mussels well,
to remove any sand, and discard any with broken shells or that
remain open when tapped.

Heat the oil in a large pan or flameproof casserole over medium
heat. Add the onion and cook for 5 minutes, or until soft.

Stir in the garlic, tomatoes, cayenne, and saffron. Season with salt
and pepper. Cook for 5 minutes, stirring occasionally.

Add the cod and the cleaned mussels. Pour in just enough water
to cover and bring to a boil. Reduce the heat to low. Cover and
simmer for 10 minutes, or until the mussels open. Discard any that
have not opened.

Add the shrimp, crab meat, and clams with their juice. Simmer
for 5 minutes more, or until the shrimp are pink.

Stir in the cilantro just before serving.

chunky cod stew
with celery & bell peppers

		ingredients	
easy		2 red bell peppers, halved and deseeded	salt and pepper
			2 celery stalks, sliced thinly
serves 4		3 tbsp olive oil	1 lb 5 oz/600 g fresh or frozen thick
		1 onion, chopped finely	cod steaks, cut into chunks
		2 garlic cloves, chopped very finely	generous ³⁄₄ cup stale coarse
35 minutes		1 tbsp white wine vinegar	bread crumbs
		1 tbsp tomato paste	8–10 black olives, pitted and sliced
		1 tbsp dried thyme or oregano	
1 hour 10 minutes		generous 1 cup fish stock	chopped celery leaves, to garnish

Place the bell peppers cut side down on a cookie sheet under a preheated hot broiler for 10–12 minutes until beginning to blacken. Heat 1 tablespoon of the olive oil in a shallow casserole. Cook the onion for 5 minutes, stirring. Add the garlic, vinegar, tomato paste, and half the thyme or oregano. Cook, stirring, for 1 minute. Add the stock. Simmer for 5 minutes.

Preheat the oven to 400°F/200°C. Remove the skin from the bell peppers. Roughly chop the flesh. Put in a blender or food processor with the onion mixture. Season with salt and pepper. Process until smooth and pour into the casserole. Add the celery and cod. Bring to a boil, then cover, and bake for 35 minutes.

Combine the bread crumbs, remaining oil, olives, remaining thyme, salt, and pepper in a small bowl. Sprinkle the mixture over the fish. Brown under a hot broiler for 5 minutes. Garnish with chopped celery leaves before serving.

monkfish ragoût

		ingredients	
easy	2 tbsp olive oil		14 oz/400 g canned
	1 small onion, chopped finely		chopped tomatoes
serves 4–6	1 red bell pepper, deseeded and cut		$^{2}/_{3}$ cup dry red wine
	into 1 inch/2.5 cm pieces		salt and pepper
	1$^{2}/_{3}$ cups thinly sliced mushrooms		1 lb 4 oz/550 g monkfish, skinned
	3 garlic cloves, chopped very finely		and cubed
35 minutes	1 tbsp tomato paste		1 yellow or green zucchini, sliced
	2 tbsp chopped fresh		
	flat leaf parsley		6–8 fresh basil leaves (shredded),
35 minutes	$^{1}/_{2}$ tsp dried oregano		to garnish

Heat the oil in a heavy pan or flameproof casserole over medium
heat. Add the onion, bell pepper, and mushrooms and cook for
5 minutes, or until beginning to soften.

Stir in the garlic, tomato paste, parsley, and oregano. Cook
together for 1 minute. Pour in the tomatoes and wine. Season
with salt and pepper. Bring the mixture to a boil, then simmer
gently for 10–15 minutes, or until slightly thickened.

Add the monkfish and the zucchini slices. Cover and simmer
for 15 minutes, or until the monkfish is cooked and the zucchini is
tender but still brightly colored.

Sprinkle with the basil just before serving.

shellfish hotpot with
red wine & tomatoes

	ingredients	
very easy	12 oz/350 g mussels, scrubbed	1 cup dry red wine
	4 tbsp olive oil	salt and pepper
serves 4–6	1 onion, chopped finely	1 lb/450 g firm white fish,
	1 green bell pepper, deseeded	such as cod or monkfish, cut into
	and chopped	2 inch/5 cm pieces
40 minutes	2 garlic cloves, chopped very finely	4 oz/115 g scallops, halved
	5 tbsp tomato paste	1 cup peeled raw shrimp
	1 tbsp chopped fresh flat leaf parsley	7 oz/200 g can crab meat
1 hour 10 minutes	1 tsp dried oregano	
	14 oz/400 g canned	10–15 fresh basil leaves, shredded,
	chopped tomatoes	to garnish

Remove the "beards" from the mussels. Rinse the mussels well, to remove any sand, and discard any with broken shells or that remain open when tapped.

Heat the oil in a large, heavy pan or flameproof casserole over medium heat. Add the onion and bell pepper. Cook for 5 minutes, or until beginning to soften.

Stir in the garlic, tomato paste, parsley, and oregano. Cook for 1 minute, stirring.

Pour in the tomatoes and wine. Season with salt and pepper. Bring to a boil, then cover, and simmer over low heat for 30 minutes. Add the fish. Cover and simmer for 15 minutes.

Add the mussels, scallops, shrimp, and crab meat. Cover and cook for 15 minutes more. Discard any mussels that have not opened.

Stir in the basil just before serving.

index